BOOK 2
Short -e

Where Is Hamm?

Published by Scholastic Inc., *Publishers since 1920*. SCHOLASTIC and associated logos
are trademarks and/or registered trademarks of Scholastic Inc. All rights reserved.

The publisher does not have any control over and does not assume
any responsibility for author or third-party websites or their content.

This book is a work of fiction. Names, characters, places, and incidents are either the product of the
author's imagination or are used fictitiously, and any resemblance to actual persons, living or dead,
business establishments, events, or locales is entirely coincidental.

ISBN: 978-1-338-57285-8

10 9 8 7 6 5 4 3 2 1   19 20 21 22 23

Printed in Malaysia   106

First printing, 2019

Book design by Marissa Asuncion

Scholastic Inc.

Woody hops off Andy's **bed**.
"Hi, Rex! Hi, Jess!" he says.
Woody looks around.
He does not see the piggy bank.
"Where is Hamm?" he says.

The toys **check** under the **bed**.
They **check** under the **desk**.
They **check** under the rug.
They **check** in the **chest**.

Where is Hamm?

The toys find some money
on Andy's **desk**.
Maybe Hamm **left** it there.

Where is Hamm?

The toys **get** together.
Maybe Hamm needs
their **help**.
What should they do **next**?
"**Let's** find Hamm," says
Woody.

The toys **set** off to
find Hamm.
Maybe he **left** a clue.
They go down the **steps**.
They look here.
They look there.

The toys find more money.
Is it a clue?
Maybe Hamm **left** it there.
What should they do?

The toys **spend** all day looking for Hamm.

When Andy **gets** home, he puts down his pack and goes out to play. Woody **checks** the pack. There is Hamm!

The toys are happy.
Their **friend** is safe.
"I **spent** the day with Andy,"
says Hamm.
"That's **swell**," says Woody.
"We're glad you're back!"